I0554665

Chinese History

500 Interesting Facts About Chinese History

© **Copyright 2023 - All rights reserved.**

The content contained within this book may not be reproduced, duplicated, or transmitted without direct written permission from the author or the publisher.

Under no circumstances will any blame or legal responsibility be held against the publisher, or author, for any damages, reparation, or monetary loss due to the information contained within this book, either directly or indirectly.

Legal Notice:

This book is copyright protected. It is only for personal use. You cannot amend, distribute, sell, use, quote, or paraphrase any part, or the content within this book, without the consent of the author or publisher.

Disclaimer Notice:

Please note the information contained within this document is for educational and entertainment purposes only. All effort has been executed to present accurate, up-to-date, reliable, and complete information. No warranties of any kind are declared or implied. Readers acknowledge that the author is not engaging in the rendering of legal, financial, medical, or professional advice. The content within this book has been derived from various sources. Please consult a licensed professional before attempting any techniques outlined in this book.

By reading this document, the reader agrees that under no circumstances is the author responsible for any losses, direct or indirect, that are incurred as a result of the use of the information contained within this document, including, but not limited to, errors, omissions, or inaccuracies.

Welcome Aboard, Check Out This Limited-Time Free Bonus!

Ahoy, reader! Welcome to the Ahoy Publications family, and thanks for snagging a copy of this book! Since you've chosen to join us on this journey, we'd like to offer you something special.

Check out the link below for a FREE e-book filled with delightful facts about American History.

But that's not all - you'll also have access to our exclusive email list with even more free e-books and insider knowledge. Well, what are ye waiting for? Visit the link below to join and set sail toward exciting adventures in American History.

To access your limited-time free bonus, go to: ahoypublications.com/

Table of Contents

Introduction

For generations, **the history of China has been a story filled with success and struggle. From pre-imperial China to the People's Republic of China**, Chinese civilization has experienced astounding accomplishments and grave challenges.

This book provides an overview of the notable periods in Chinese history, from **the Qin dynasty** to **China's Open Door Policy**. In each chapter, we will explore the cultural and political landscape of China through dynasties like **the Han** and **Southern Song** and through tumultuous events like **the Opium Wars** and **the Taiping Rebellion.**

We will also examine some of **the pivotal moments in modern Chinese history**, including **Yuan Shikai's** attempt to reestablish imperial rule, **the Chinese Civil War, the Cultural Revolution, the Tiananmen Square protests**, and the rise of China as a superpower. Throughout this book, we will take a close look at notable milestones and small details that give insight into how these periods shaped modern culture.

By reading about history, we gain a better understanding of cultures and modern-day events. **This is an adventure into the past** that will not only enlighten us but also captivate our imaginations and leave us eager to explore even more.

Pre-Imperial China
(ca. 2000–221 BCE)

This chapter will explore the fascinating history of pre-imperial China with thirty interesting facts. With this insight into pre-imperial Chinese society, we can gain a greater appreciation for its sophistication and resilience during this time in history.

1. **Pre-imperial China** lasted from about 2000 BCE to 221 BCE.

2. During this time, **the Chinese people spoke many different languages** and followed different customs, depending on where they lived in China.

3. The dominant group during pre-imperial times was **the Zhou dynasty (1046–256 BCE)**.

4. **The Chinese developed complex systems of government**, law, and writing that lasted for centuries after the pre-imperial period ended.

5. **Pre-imperial Chinese society was split into classes** based on wealth, power, and ancestry.

6. **Farmers provided food to feed everyone**. Millet was one of the most important crops in ancient China.

7. Effectively **managing water resources became an integral part of daily life** due to the frequent flooding of nearby rivers. With the help of wealthy landlords, who often owned large tracts of land alongside rivers, **the Chinese** were able to build irrigation systems.

8. **Confucius was a famous Chinese philosopher** who lived during pre-imperial times. His teachings on morality, justice, and respect were highly influential in imperial China. They still continue to shape Chinese society to a large degree today.

9. During this period, **some of the earliest forms of martial arts emerged**. Probably dating back to **the Xia dynasty about four thousand years ago**, the main use of martial arts was for self-defense and hunting.

10. **The Silk Road was an overland trade route connecting Asia to Europe.** It had multiple routes that ran **from China through central Asia to the West**. While evidence of trade via **the Silk Road** during pre-imperial times has been discovered in various parts of Eurasia, the trade route would become far more cohesive in the 2nd century BCE.

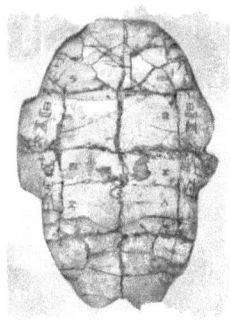

11. **The earliest Chinese writing comes from the pre-imperial era**. A pictographic script known as *jiaguwen* **has been found on animal bones and turtle shells** dating back to about 1200 BCE.

12. Objects from **early Bronze Age tombs reveal that people knew astronomy and mathematics**. Archeologists have discovered lacquer boxes containing names of tens of lunar mansions (divisions of the sky), dating back to the 5th century BCE.

13. **The construction of walls that later joined to form the Great Wall started in the 7th century BCE.** The walls were meant to defend the Chinese lands from northern invaders. They were built partially from stone, wood, and rammed earth.

14. **Different sections of the Great Wall were added throughout the centuries**. The final sections of the wall were completed during **the Ming dynasty (1368–1644 CE)**, meaning that it took more than **two thousand years to finish the Great Wall!**

15. **Chinese invented primitive compasses** around the 4th century BCE. These compasses weren't used to find the way north. **They were used to find the right direction in life.** These compasses were **used in rituals, feng shui practices, and fortune-telling.**

16. **Philosophical schools** of thought such as **Daoism, Confucianism, and Mohism** heavily influenced pre-imperial China.

17. **Ancient Chinese believed in ancestor worship**. They would honor their ancestors with offerings of food or incense placed on altars.

18. **Bronze vessels and weapons were common during pre-imperial times**. These objects often had intricate designs etched into them.

19. **The earliest coins developed in East Asia came from the Zhou dynasty (1046–256 BCE).** However, no developed monetary system existed, and the coins did not look like the coins we use today. Instead, things found in nature, like cowrie shells, were frequently used.

20. **An interesting discovery dating back to pre-imperial China is oracle bones.** Bones were inscribed with important questions on weather or battles and then were heated up until they produced cracks. **The patterns provided by the cracks were then interpreted by oracles.**

21. **Tea drinking became popular in parts of China during the Zhou dynasty**. Although it was **first used for medicinal purposes**, the nobility started to pick up tea drinking as a luxury activity.

22. **Ancient Chinese people developed some of the earliest forms of pottery and ceramics.** They used these items for cooking, storage, and burial.

23. **Traditional Chinese medicine has been practiced since pre-imperial times**. Healers would use herbs and acupuncture techniques to treat illnesses.

24. **Thought to exist from around 2000 to 1600 BCE, the semi-mythical Xia dynasty is considered to be one of the first** (if not the first) **ruling dynasties of ancient China.** It is commonly held that the first Xia ruler by the name of Yu was the first to obtain the divine right to rule, also known as the Mandate of Heaven.

25. **Pre-imperial China saw an exceptional advancement in metallurgy.** Iron tools and weapons slowly replaced bronze toward the end of the 6th century BCE in the Yangtse Valley. Iron would become the preferred metal of choice around 300 BCE.

26. **Perhaps the most famous piece of literature written during the pre-imperial era is** *The Art of War* **by military strategist Sun Tzu.** The book was written sometime in the 5th century BCE and remains a popular military treatise to this day.

27. Other classics, like **the late 9th-century BCE** *I Ching* (*Book of Changes*) and **the 5th-century BCE** *Tao Te Ching* (*Book of the Way*), were also composed during this era.

28. **One of the most fundamental ideas of ancient Chinese culture is yin and yang, a concept that states everything has two opposite yet interconnected sides.** Although these terms weren't used in the pre-imperial era, there is evidence that the idea behind yin and yang was starting to form.

29. **The pre-imperial era saw the first few iterations of Chinese calendars.** The ancient Chinese used solar calendars. **During the Zhou dynasty, the Chinese used a lunisolar calendar.**

30. **Pre-imperial China saw exceptional advances in mathematics**. They developed math independently (meaning they weren't influenced by other civilizations) during the 11th century BCE.

Qin Dynasty
(221–206 BCE)

Discover the fascinating history of the Qin dynasty, China's first imperial dynasty. We'll discover how **Emperor Qin Shi Huang created a unified Chinese empire** with these ten amazing facts!

31. **The Qin Dynasty was the first dynasty in the Chinese imperial era**. It lasted from 221 to 206 BCE.

32. **Emperor Qin Shi Huang conquered the six Zhou warring states**, unifying them into one country with a single government.

33. **He is also known for uniting the already-existing walls into the Great Wall of China** to protect his kingdom from invaders.

34. **During the Qin dynasty**, technology was significantly advanced. **Crossbows were used more often in warfare**, and **iron plows helped farmers grow crops** more effectively.

35. You might have heard of **the Terracotta Army. It was built to "guard" the tomb of Emperor Qin Shi Huang**. It consists of over eight thousand life-sized clay soldiers. These soldiers were all buried alongside the emperor in a secret underground complex near the city of Xi'an in central China.

36. At its peak, **the population of the Qin dynasty had tens of millions of people under its rule.**

37. **Emperor Qin Shi Huang created a standardized system for money** and weights and measures, which unified China's economy.

38. **A large number of books were burned and destroyed during his reign**. The emperor wanted to discourage people from learning about different ideas or teachings that he disapproved of, **such as Confucianism**. He even buried hundreds of Confucian scholars alive!

39. **The Chinese legal code was established during this period** and would be used for hundreds of years in the future; it focused mainly on values such as filial piety (respecting your parents).

40. **This dynasty lasted only fifteen years, but its cultural impact cannot be denied**. The Qin Empire standardized writing, expanded roads, and created a better postal system.

Han Dynasty
(202 BCE–220 CE)

Explore **the fascinating history of the Han dynasty**. Find out **how Confucianism became an official ideology during this period** and what impact it had on Chinese society. Also, explore the cultural exchange that took place due to **the Silk Road**. You might be surprised to learn what was traded!

41. **The Han dynasty was the second imperial dynasty of China** and lasted from 202 BCE to 220 CE.

42. **Liu Bang, better known as Emperor Gaozu, founded the dynasty** after he defeated his rival, **Xiang Yu**, the leader of **the rebel forces that overthrew the Qin dynasty**, in 202 BCE.

43. **Chinese culture flourished with advances in literature, art, music, and technology.** For example, in 132 CE, the Chinese invented an early form of a **seismograph for detecting earthquakes.**

44. **Confucianism**, which helped shape government policies and social values throughout East Asia, **became the official state ideology.**

45. **Chang'an** (modern-day Xi'an) **was the capital of the Han dynasty** for about the first two hundred years.

46. **Trade between China and other countries increased significantly during this period** due to improved transportation networks like canals or roads.

47. **The Silk Road trade routes were officially established, connecting China with central Asia, India, the Middle East, and Europe.** These routes were used for centuries by merchants traveling between countries with goods like silk, spices, and tea.

48. **The Han dynasty was divided into two periods**: Western Han (202 BCE–9 CE) and **Eastern Han** (25–220 CE).

49. **Emperor Wu of the Western Han is considered one of China's greatest rulers**. He expanded the borders to include parts of central Asia, Korea, and Vietnam.

50. **A civil service exam system was established** to allow people from all social classes to become government officials based on their knowledge instead of their birthright or wealth.

51. **The monetary system, which had been profoundly developed during the Qin dynasty, was further advanced**. New coins were added to make transactions easier.

52. **The first Chinese compass is thought to have been invented during the Han dynasty.** Originally called the **"south-pointing fish,"** it was not used for navigation but rather for fortune-telling and choosing building sites.

53. **Buddhism first arrived in China during the Eastern Han** period when **it spread from India through the Silk Road.** Traders brought scriptures back home with them after visiting foreign lands like Tibet or Nepal. Ideas and cultural aspects were traded just as much as goods!

54. **Emperor Wu sent a diplomat by the name of Zhang Qian to explore central Asia** and establish better trade routes in the 2nd century. He would quickly emerge as one of the most famous travelers.

55. **Zhang Qian also brought back knowledge that helped improve agriculture in China,** such as new crops like grapes and pomegranates.

56. **The Chinese social classes went through an interesting transformation during the Han period,** with the farmers rising in importance while merchants were considered to have been a lower class.

57. **Thanks to the opening of many new trade routes, advancements were made in Chinese medicine**, with doctors using acupuncture for injuries and the treatment of illnesses more akin to how we would today.

58. **The Great Wall of China was extended farther westward** during this era to protect against nomadic invasions from central Asian tribes like **the Xiongnu or Huns**, who threatened China's borders.

59. **The most recognizable parts of the Great Wall were built during the Han dynasty.**

60. **The Han dynasty used the decimal system** for counting and measuring.

61. **The Han also discovered square roots and cube roots!**

62. From 9 to 23 CE, **the Han dynasty was overthrown by the Xin dynasty**. After the Han dynasty was restored in 25 CE, Han rule was referred to as the Eastern Han.

63. Chinese literature flourished, with authors like **historian Sima Qian and historian/poet Ban Gu**. Their works are still being read and studied by people today.

64. **Zhang Heng, a famous Chinese astronomer**, noted around 2,500 stars and more than one hundred constellations!

65. **Artisans created beautiful pieces of pottery decorated** with intricate designs using glazes made from minerals found in nearby mountainsides or rivers.

66. Despite merchants' relatively low social status, **the merchant class managed to grow its wealth thanks to a lot of new trading routes.**

67. **Papermaking was invented during this time**. It was likely made using mulberry bark fibers, hemp, and rags. The invention of paper revolutionized communication.

68. **The Han dynasty is credited with inventing fireworks**, though its design differed greatly from later iterations of fireworks with gunpowder. People simply heated up bamboo sticks until they would sizzle and cause the air inside them to explode. For this reason, they were **called *baozhu* or "exploding bamboo."**

69. **Emperor Wu established an imperial university where students could study Confucianism**, literature, and other topics to become educated officials for government positions.

70. **The Han Dynasty started to decline after the death of Emperor Ling in 189 AD**. The instability created after the death of the emperor eventually caused the collapse of the dynasty after about thirty years of internal fighting.

Period of the Three Kingdoms
(220–280 CE)

Discover how different kingdoms fought for control over China, and learn about some of the legendary figures from this time, like **Cao Cao, Liu Bei, and Sun Quan.** Our twenty interesting facts will show you why this period is still remembered today!

71. **The Three Kingdoms was a time of chaos and war in ancient China,** lasting from 220 to 280 CE.

72. **The collapse of the Eastern Han dynasty led to the period of the Three Kingdoms,** with warlords fighting over control of China.

73. Three different kingdoms formed during this period: **Cao Wei, Shu Han, and Eastern Wu.** These kingdoms helped establish some semblance of peace.

74. Many **great generals** fought with each other for control over ancient China. **Cao Cao, Liu Bei, and Sun Quan** are just some examples.

75. **Cao Cao was a prominent statesman and warlord during the final years of the Han dynasty.** As one of the most influential figures of **the Three Kingdoms period,** he used his influence to create his own separate state named **Cao Wei** (or just Wei), though he never actually declared himself emperor.

76. **Liu Bei, another general of the Eastern Han dynasty, created his own state of Shu Han,** which was southwest of Cao Cao's Wei.

77. Another legendary figure from **the Three Kingdoms period was Zhuge Liang,** an incredibly wise strategist and advisor to **Liu Bei's army.**

78. Younger than his rivals Cao Cao and Liu Bei, the third most important warlord and ruler of the third of **the Three Kingdoms was Sun Quan.** He ruled the southern and eastern parts of China, which were organized into **the Kingdom of Wu.**

79. Eventually, prominent **general and politician Sima Yi gained power and orchestrated a coup d'état in Cao Wei,** emerging as the de facto ruler of the state from 249 to 251 before founding his own dynasty.

80. Many **famous warriors** became known for their skill and bravery, such as **Guan Yu and Zhang Fei!**

81. **The Three Kingdoms was a bloody period**, but Cao Cao and his sons were actually renowned poets!

82. In 260 CE, **the kingdom of Shu Han was defeated by the kingdom of Cao Wei**. Cao Wei would rule until **the Jin dynasty** took over in 266 CE.

83. Many great battles took place during this period. **The Battle of Red Cliffs**, which took place about twelve years before the start of **the Three Kingdoms** period, saw **Liu Bei and Sun Quan defeat Cao Cao's much larger army with clever tactics**. This battle helped decide the borders of two of the three kingdoms.

84. **The Three Kingdoms contested each other for power**, and their rulers all claimed the Mandate of Heaven—**the divine right to rule—at the same time**. While they were culturally and socially almost identical, there was no one "true" political entity of China during this time.

85. In 263, **the Kingdom of Shu Han fell. In 266, Sima Yan forced the ruler of the Kingdom of Wei to abdicate**. He created a new dynasty called Jin and became Emperor Wu of Jin.

86. **In 280, the Jin conquered Eastern Wu, unifying all of China under one banner.**

87. In the late 3rd century, about a decade after all of China had been unified, a series of internal conflicts, known as **the War of the Eight Princes**, helped bring about **the Jin dynasty's decline.**

88. **The Jin dynasty did not retain control for long**, lasting for less than 150 years. The dynasty fell to **the Song dynasty** in 420.

89. **Since the Three Kingdoms was a very exciting period**, the era is still remembered today through many TV shows, movies, books, and computer games.

90. **One of the most famous Chinese novels, *Romance of the Three Kingdoms*, is based on** events that happened during this period.

Sixteen Kingdoms
(304–439 CE)

Explore **the fascinating history of China** during the period of **the Sixteen Kingdoms**. Discover why warlords fought each other while also unifying cultures. **Learn about powerful kingdoms,** and uncover how this period of fighting ended with these thirty interesting facts!

91. **The Sixteen Kingdoms was a chaotic time in Chinese history** that lasted from 304 to 439 CE.

92. The Sixteen Kingdoms period is interesting for historians because **it is one of the first large-scale conflicts in Chinese history** that was motivated by ethnic divisions to a large extent.

93. It began after the collapse of **the Western Jin dynasty** and ended with **the reunification of Northern China** in 439 by the Northern Wei.

94. **When the Western Jin dynasty collapsed, the Eastern Jin dynasty was established**. It ruled over southern China.

95. Despite its power, **it eventually collapsed due to a series of internal conflicts between rival factions** within the royal court and external invasions.

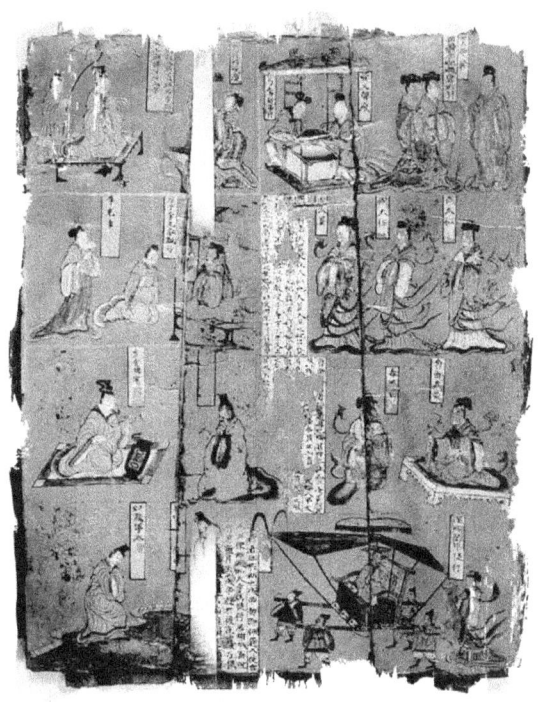

96. **In 291, a series of wars known as the War of the Eight Princes began**. Different princes and kings sought power over the Western Jin dynasty, which significantly weakened the dynasty and allowed other kingdoms to become more powerful at its expense.

97. **The Western Jin dynasty is important** for many reasons. For instance, it began to see **the Sinicization of non-Chinese people** who settled in the lands. This wasn't a state-run program, although that would happen later in **Chinese history**.

98. During the Sixteen Kingdoms period, **China was divided into several kingdoms ruled by different warlords**. These men constantly fought each other for control over territory and resources.

99. Although it is called **the Sixteen Kingdoms**, more than sixteen kingdoms emerged. Some kingdoms were just stronger than others.

100. Some historians believe **there were at least twenty-two "independent" political entities in China during this period**, ranging from smaller provinces to full-scale empires.

101. **States rose and fell**, which means these kingdoms were not fighting each other all at the same time.

102. Even though **each kingdom was politically independent**, the basis of their culture and traditions was mostly the same, though unique circumstances would sometimes lead to the development of different practices.

103. **The political instability led to massive population movements within China**, as people sought refuge from the conflicts between warring states.

104. **Sima Yan, the founder of the Jin dynasty**, was notorious for giving his family members a lot of power, something that ultimately contributed to the breakout of **the War of the Eight Princes.**

105. **There were many great military strategists during** this era. **Shi Le,** who once was a slave, rose up to become the leader of his own dynasty, **the Later Zhou.** Although **he is seen as a brilliant military mind,** he was unnecessarily cruel in his campaigns.

106. **Confucianism remained a staple philosophy during this era.**

107. **Buddhism also spread during this period**. Many monasteries were built in various cities across China.

108. **Yao Xing, ruler of the Later Qin dynasty, was a devoted Buddhist.** During his reign, Buddhism received official state support for the first time in China.

109. **The first Buddhist grottoes** (or caves) were carved during this period. It is believed **there were over one thousand caves in the Mogao cave system**. Today, there are over seven hundred Mogao caves. The ones built during the Sixteen Kingdoms have largely been lost.

110. Despite its political instability, **the Sixteen Kingdoms was a significant era for Chinese culture,** as it brought together different cultures and allowed people to exchange ideas.

111. **Cui Hong, a 6th-century historian, was the first person to use the term "Sixteen Kingdoms" in his writings.**

112. A contributing **factor to the collapse of the Western Jin dynasty was the immigration of the "Five Barbarian" clans**, who arrived in northern China during the late Eastern Han dynasty. Eventually, they played a role in overthrowing the Jin and organized their own states.

113. Coming mostly from modern-day Mongolia and central Asia, **the Five Barbarian tribes were not ethnically Chinese and lived nomadic lifestyles.**

114. **These non-Chinese peoples would eventually partially adopt Chinese customs and traditions**, especially when it came to administration and governance.

115. Literature from this period includes the works of **Tao Yuanming, a renowned poet also known as Tao Qian.** He wrote about everyday life in his native Fujian Province.

116. Among the newly established kingdoms, the only one that was able to unify a significant chunk of land for a longer time was **the Northern Wei, founded by the Tuoba people in 386 CE.**

117. Interestingly, because many of **the newly arrived foreign clans embraced Buddhism,** it spread as a prominent religion throughout northern China during this period.

118. **The Northern Wei chose Luoyang as its capital.** Having served as an ancient imperial capital, this choice was conscious, demonstrating the will of **the Tuoba to legitimize themselves and assimilate with the Chinese culture and people.**

119. **Culturally, this period of turmoil was not entirely stagnant as one might expect.** The discovery of terracotta statues dated to the Sixteen Kingdoms proves this.

120. **One famous battle during this time was the Battle of Fei River,** where two armies clashed on opposite sides of a river near modern-day Hefei.

The Period of the Northern and Southern Dynasties
(420–589 CE)

Explore **the rich history of the Northern and Southern dynasties** with us! This chapter will cover twenty astonishing facts about this era. Although **it was another chaotic time in history,** it also saw the rise of the arts. **Discover how religion, trade, and warfare shaped the culture of this era** and how great generals and poets left their mark on Chinese history.

121. **The Northern and Southern dynasties** saw the north and south of China separated into two separate kingdoms.

122. **Northern China was home to the Northern Wei**, which later split into the Eastern and Western Wei. **Northern Qi and Northern Zhou** would come at the tail end of this period.

123. **Southern China saw the rise of Liu Song**, Southern Qi, Liang, and Chen. These kingdoms did not coexist with each other.

124. **Despite being rivals from the beginning, neither one of the Northern and Southern dynasties managed to emerge as the most powerful entity in China.**

125. **During this period, Buddhism grew in popularity. Daoism** (or Taoism) was also embraced by the people.

126. **Many Buddhist temples were built during this era.** Some of these temples still exist, such as **the Shaolin Temple in** Henan Province or **the Yungang Grottoes** near Datong in Shanxi Province.

127. **Buddhist monasteries existed in parts of northern China**. There, monks would teach others about their religion while also **providing medical care**, education, and other forms of humanitarian aid.

128. **A big focus during this period was on paintings and sculptures**, which sometimes featured Buddhas.

129. **Poets wrote beautiful works about nature** inspired by the beauty they saw while traveling around rural areas throughout China. **Yu Xin and Wei Shou** are some notable examples.

130. **Emperor Wu of Liang**, ruling in the first half of the 6th century, was a notable patron of the arts.

131. **Many forms of arts were pursued**, most notably music and calligraphy, the latter of which had emerged as a very respectable art form.

132. **Prominent families dominated the power struggles in the Southern dynasties,** thanks in part to the powers attributed to the family clansmen by Cao Cao in the past.

133. **The Silk Road was still an essential part of the economy**, as it allowed merchants to transport goods from China to Europe with relative ease. This resulted in cultural exchanges between different countries, which helped spread knowledge about foreign lands.

134. **Advances were made in mathematics**, like calculating pi with more accuracy or developing new methods for solving algebraic equations.

135. **The Northern and Southern dynasties saw the introduction of new taxation,** coinage, and currency systems.

136. **The period witnessed a significant rise in trade with other countries**, which helped strengthen the Chinese economy through increased wealth and imported resources from abroad.

137. Much like during earlier periods, **the main power lay in the hands of generals and warlords,** who used the loyalty of their troops to rise to power and establish their own dominions.

138. During this period, **the non-Han (ethnically Chinese)** peoples who had migrated to northern China and had later risen to power, like **the Xianbei** and **the Tuoba**, became more and more assimilated with the Chinese culture to be more fit to rule their Chinese subjects.

139. **Landscape paintings became very popular in China** due to their vivid colors and excellent brushstrokes, capturing the beauty of nature with great detail.

140. **The Northern and Southern dynasties ended after Emperor Wen of the Sui dynasty declared himself ruler of all of China,** unifying both northern and southern parts under his reign in 589.

Sui Dynasty
(581–618 CE)

This chapter will **explore the fascinating Sui dynasty**, which lasted from 581 to 618 CE. Examine an array of interesting facts about the period and its key figures, including **Emperor Wen and his son Yang Guang**. We will also look at aspects of **Chinese culture** and how they impacted the next dynasty, the famous Tang dynasty.

141. **The Sui dynasty was a Chinese imperial dynasty** that lasted a short time, from 581 to 618 CE.

142. **Yang Jian, who took the name Emperor Wen,** founded the dynasty and later became its first emperor.

143. During this period, **essential infrastructure projects were built, such as canals, roads, and bridges,** to help expand transportation and trade in China.

144. **To build these projects, the Sui government conscripted workers.** This move led to tensions, as the people had to deal with conscription and heavy taxation.

145. **Emperor Wen improved education during his reign** by introducing a national civil service examination system, which helped people get jobs in the government based on their abilities rather than family connections or wealth.

146. **One of the most notable achievements from this era was the Grand Canal.** It linked the northern and southern parts of China, helping to unify the country.

147. **Sections of the Great Wall were repaired during the Sui dynasty** to provide more safety to the northern part of China.

148. **The Sui dynasty promoted Buddhism throughout its reign**, with Chinese schools of Buddhist thought becoming more prominent. It is thought that the flourishment of Buddhism allowed the Chinese culture to reemerge stronger than ever.

149. **Emperor Wen was succeeded by his son Yang Guang (Emperor Yang),** who began to rule in 604 CE. **Emperor Yang was known for his extravagance** and lavish lifestyle, which significantly weakened the dynasty's finances.

150. **Japan was a strong trade partner of the Sui dynasty**, while Korea and Vietnam were among the two chief external enemies of China at the time.

151. In 617 CE, **General Li Yuan led a successful coup against Emperor Yang due to anger over high taxes**, which eventually resulted in the overthrow of the Sui dynasty in favor of **the Tang dynasty**, beginning a new era of prosperity under their rule.

152. During this period, **Chinese culture flourished with painting, music, and literature**.

153. Interestingly, **the last Sui emperor and Emperor Wen's successor, Yang Guang, was also one of the most renowned poets of this period.**

154. **Emperor Wen, who devoted a lot of funds to the military,** managed to assemble a force that was several hundred thousand men strong and marched them to **battle against the Chen on the Yangtze River.**

155. **The Sui military campaigns against Vietnam were partially successful.** Northern Vietnam was retaken (it had been under the control of the Chinese during the Han and Jin dynasties), but further pushes into the south were abandoned due to difficulties that the Chinese armies encountered.

156. Despite **the Sui dynasty's** relatively short rule, it made many lasting contributions that shaped China, such as **the Kaihuang Code**. This law code got rid of harsher punishments and replaced them with punishments that were more accepted by the people. These punishments are harsh by today's standards, but being banished or beaten with a big stick sounds a lot better than being torn limb from limb!

157. **The Tang dynasty didn't change much of what the Sui dynasty had established.** For instance, the Tang rulers based their laws **on the Kaihuang Code**.

158. **The ambitious and lavish endeavors of the Sui emperors eventually greatly depleted the dynasty's finances,** contributing to its relatively quick decline.

159. **The war with the Korean Kingdom of Goguryeo was deadly**. None of the four expeditions the Sui launched ended in success.

160. **The fall of the Sui dynasty marked the end of a brief** but influential period that helped shape China's future, especially in regard to culture and religion.

Tang Dynasty
(618–907 CE)

The Tang dynasty is considered one of the more well-known dynasties of China. It saw the flourishing of culture and advancements in technology. You might be shocked to learn what was discovered during this time, and you might be even more shocked to learn that **we use many of those inventions still!**

161. **The Tang dynasty started in 618 and ended in 907 CE.** There was a brief break in the empire, lasting from 690 to 705.

162. **During the Tang dynasty, Chinese culture flourished** with advancements like printing, a form of paper money, and the creation of gunpowder.

163. **The capital city during this period was Chang'an** (now known as Xi'an).

164. **One of the greatest rulers of the dynasty was Emperor Taizong.** His reforms and achievements increased China's prosperity and stability during his reign, which lasted from 626 to 649.

165. **The Tang dynasty is known as the Buddhist golden age.** Although **most of the emperors were Daoists,** they greatly supported Buddhism, with the government having control over monasteries.

166. **Women had more rights than before.** They could engage in political discussions and were no longer required to wear long dresses or cover their faces.

167. **The relative period of stability under the Tang made the Silk Road trade routes much more active,** with more reliable routes being established and maintained.

168. **The most famous poet of the Tang dynasty was Li Bai,** who wrote about patriotism and nature in a spiritual manner.

169. **The Tang Dynasty reached its golden age under Emperor Xuanzong** (685-762), which was marked by economic and political stability and prosperity.

170. **Emperor Xuanzong was also admired for his patronage of the arts and education,** which attracted a lot of poets, philosophers, and artists to his court.

171. Unlike in the past, **the Great Wall of China was not extended** to any great length during the Tang dynasty

172. **Buddhism started to be used for political purposes by rulers like Empress Wu Zetian,** who declared herself an enlightened ruler supported by Buddhist doctrine.

173. To assert her dominance, **Wu Zetian introduced new characters for a brief period of time into the written language,** though the changes were reversed after her death.

174. **The Tang dynasty saw a precursor to Chinese opera called *canjunxi* become popular.** *Canjunxi* originated from folk music, and *canjunxi* later told concise stories.

175. **The invention of gunpowder is attributed to Chinese monks and alchemists during this period.** Gunpowder is believed to have been invented around 850. It eventually spread to Europe via contacts with merchants on the Silk Road.

176. **Tea became popular among all classes** due to its medicinal properties and was exported abroad as far away as Japan.

177. **The Tang dynasty is known for its ceramics**, many of which have been found in archaeological sites around the world.

178. **Martial arts, such as Shaolin kung fu, took off during this time.** Martial arts were practiced for health benefits and self-defensive purposes.

179. **The population increased significantly throughout the dynasty** from an estimated fifty million people at its start to perhaps around seventy-five million by 900 CE.

180. **The use of umbrellas became more common during the Tang dynasty.** People used them to protect their clothing from rain, but umbrellas were also used to provide shade from the sun.

181. **Painting flourished with notable artists, such as Wu Daozi and Zhang Xuan,** painting on silk, wooden boards, walls, and ceilings.

182. The recently established Imperial Examination System was expanded and used more commonly during the Tang times, contributing to the creation of a new class of ruling elites. Still, as the system was still relatively new, it took the Chinese civil servants a bit of time to adapt to it.

183. Pancakes became quite popular during the Tang dynasty. Eating beef, on the other hand, was discouraged.

184. The first recorded Christian missionary arrived in China in 635.

185. Eunuchs became notable figures in court due to their closeness to the emperor, with some achieving significant influence over policy-making decisions.

186. Stability and the flourishing of the Silk Road trade routes allowed new goods, practices, and fashions to enter China for the first time after a long era of turmoil

187. Domestic trade routes also developed, thanks to the repairs done to the Grand Canal.

188. The Tang dynasty was a period of great cultural exchange, with many foreign diplomats, traders, and missionaries from as far away as Japan, India, and Persia bringing their ideas and beliefs to China.

189. Establishing diplomatic relations with other nations like Korea led to increased trade between them, such as the export of silk cloths or lacquerware.

190. Although **the Tang dynasty launched military campaigns,** they were not as successful as previous dynasties.

The Five Dynasties and Ten Kingdoms Period
(907–960 CE)

Let's go from **the golden age of the Tang dynasty** to another chaotic time in Chinese history. Discover fifteen fascinating facts about **the Five Dynasties and Ten Kingdoms period!**

191. **The Five Dynasties and Ten Kingdoms period** was a time of political fragmentation in China, lasting from 907 to 960 CE.

192. **During this period, five dynasties ruled over northern China** one after the other, and more than **twelve independent kingdoms** (together known as the Ten Kingdoms) ruled the south, often at the same time.

193. **All of these political entities based their political structures on the preceding Tang dynasty.**

194. Although this was a chaotic time, **Buddhism was still promoted**, especially in the south.

195. **One might assume that the economy declined since China was facing internal wars, but it actually saw economic growth!**

196. **The Five Dynasties of the North were Later Liang, Later Tang, Later Xin, Later Han, and Later Zhou.**

197. **They all succeeded each other** from 907 to 960, occupying the same territory and plagued with instability and warfare.

198. **The Five Dynasties and Ten Kingdoms period** ended in 960 when the Song dynasty unified China under one rule.

199. **The Ten Kingdoms**, on the other hand, were located in the southern part of China. They included **Yang Wu** (907–937), **Wuyue** (907–978), **Min** (909–945), **Ma Chu** (907–951), **Southern Han** (917–971), **Former Shu** (907–925), **Later Shu** (934–965), **Jingnan** (924–963), **Southern Tang** (937–976), and **Northern Han** (951–979).

200. Unlike **the Five Dynasties** of the north, some of **the Ten Kingdoms** existed together for brief periods of time, overlapping with each other.

201. Due to this, it is considered that **southern China was much more stable** than the north during this period.

202. Prominent artists from this period include **Li Cheng and Xu Xi**, whose artistic styles place a big emphasis on the depiction of nature as a sacred entity.

203. **This period of divide in the north ended with the Song dynasty's** reunification of northern China in 960.

204. **Serious political divides between the north and the south were expressed in the development of strong regional identities,** some of which would last for long periods of time.

205. **The period of the Five Dynasties and Ten Kingdoms** is another example of an era of strong political divide in China, exemplifying the cyclical nature of Chinese history.

Liao Dynasty
(907–1125 CE)

The Liao dynasty existed alongside the Five Dynasties and Ten Kingdoms, as well as the Song dynasty, earning it a spot in the history books. This section **will explore the history and culture of this intriguing empire** through twenty amazing facts.

206. **The Liao dynasty was founded by the Khitan people** in 907 and lasted until 1125.

207. At its height, **the dynasty ruled northern China, Mongolia**, northern **Korea**, and parts of **Russia**.

208. **The Khitan people came from the steppes of Mongolia**. They expanded in the 9th century and eventually declared themselves to be a dynastic state of China.

209. **The Khitans had been known to the Chinese for centuries**. Their earliest mention in Chinese sources appears in **the *Book of Wei***, which was completed in the 6th century.

210. **Buddhism was the most popular religion**, although the Liao religion blended Buddhism with the tribal religion, **Confucianism**, and **Daoism**.

211. **The Liao had a strong military with cavalry units that protected their borders** from invaders, like **the Song dynasty** to the south or nomadic tribes from central Asia.

212. **Their economy relied heavily on trade along the Silk Road** routes, which connected them with other cultures across Eurasia.

213. **They developed a writing system known as Khitan small script**, which allowed them to keep records of taxes or laws passed by rulers.

214. If there is a small script, there has to be a large script. Both **Khitan scripts were based on the Chinese script.**

215. The Liao emperors could read Chinese, which likely proved helpful to them. **Some Chinese works were translated into Khitan,** but it is not known for sure what. It is likely that **the Confucian classics were never translated.**

216. Khitan women enjoyed greater freedoms. For instance, women were taught how to hunt and could even manage property when their husbands were away.

217. **Liao dynasty art was varied,** but the dynasty is best remembered for its **sculptures.**

218. **No one knows for sure where the term Liao comes from.** Some believe it might come from the **Khitan word for iron.**

219. **The Liao dynasty might have used gunpowder weapons in battles.**

220. The later **Liao empire is remembered for its religious tolerance** and openness to different cultures.

221. **Administration in the lands controlled by the Liao dynasty was split into two.** One part was focused on **the Khitan population,** which was mostly concentrated in the northern part of the empire, while the southern one focused on **the Han Chinese population.**

222. **The army of the Liao was divided into different sections.** The most elite corps was comprised **of Khitan heavy cavalry,** while **the ethnic Chinese usually were the militia.**

223. **The Liao dynasty did not have a significant naval presence.** Instead, it depended on land armies to fend off enemies.

224. **In 1125, the Liao dynasty was conquered by the Jurchens,** who founded **the Jin dynasty** in its place.

225. **After the dynasty fell in 1125, some of its territories were absorbed by the Song or Jin dynasty,** while others became independent states ruled by nomadic tribes from central Asia, such as **Qara Khitai.**

Song Dynasty
[960–1279 CE]

This chapter will explore **the incredible history of the Song dynasty, one of the most prosperous periods in Chinese history**. Examine its advances in technology and art to see how its culture is still influential today.

226. **The Song dynasty lasted from 960 to 1279 and is divided into two periods: Northern Song and Southern Song.** The Southern Song dynasty was founded in 1127 and lasted until 1279.

227. **Zhao Kuangyin** (later known as **Emperor Taizu) founded the Song dynasty** after staging a coup to end **the Later Zhou dynasty**, which was the last of **the Five Dynasties**.

228. **China had one of its most prosperous periods during the Song dynasty** with advances in science and technology. **The population increased dramatically**, and the arts flourished.

229. **The first recorded chemical formula of gunpowder dates to this period**, which led to new weapons like cannons and firearms being used for warfare.

230. **Kaifeng was the Northern Song's capital city** during this period. It was located on the Yellow River. **The Southern Song's capital was Lin'an** (today's Hangzhou).

231. **The Song dynasty was the first Chinese dynasty to establish a permanent standing navy**, which allowed it to emerge as a powerful maritime power.

232. **Neo-Confucianism emerged as an influential philosophy**, emphasizing personal morality over politics or religion. **Neo-Confucianists wanted to bring back the Confucianism of old**, as the philosophy had mixed with other religions over the centuries.

233. **True north was discovered for the first time by using a compass.**

234. Important advancements were made in sanitation and urban hygiene. For example, **the Song dynasty built free public toilets in big cities.**

235. **These public toilets actually sold fecal matter to farmers.** Farms used the poop as fertilizer!

236. **Women were still seen as being lower than men on the social ladder**, but they were given more rights than before. Under special circumstances, a woman could own some of her father's property if he died.

237. **Foot binding became popular among upper-class women** who wanted smaller feet since they were seen as more graceful.

238. **The Song dynasty was the first to invent a movable printing press.** The moving pieces were made of porcelain.

239. **New star catalogs were created by astronomers like Su Song.** He also invented a water-powered armillary sphere, which tracked celestial movements accurately over time.

240. **The Song dynasty introduced the mariner's compass,** which allowed sailors to navigate more accurately.

241. During this period, Chinese literature flourished with famous poets like **Su Shi, who wrote about his travels in China, and Li Qingzhao, who wrote romantic poems** about love and nature.

242. **Art during this time included landscapes and portrait paintings. Calligraphy was another major art** form during the Song dynasty.

243. **This dynasty saw a growth in trade with other countries** like Japan and Korea through its port city Quanzhou (then known as Zaiton).

244. **Chinese porcelain became popular globally** due to its high quality and intricate designs.

245. **Tea drinking was popular during this time**, as it was a way to socialize with friends or family members over tea ceremonies.

246. **This dynasty saw increased literacy rates among men and women** due to improved education systems throughout China.

247. **Hangzhou's West Lake was a most famous tourist attraction during this era**, and it still exists today! It has been praised by many poets throughout history for its beauty and tranquility.

248. **Xiangqi, which is a Chinese version of chess, and the board game Go became popular.** These games were played recreationally and competitively.

249. After a series of political rivalries weakened the Northern Song by the 11th century, **the Northern Song was overthrown by the Jurchens, who would establish the Jin dynasty** in 1127.

250. **The Mongol Empire eventually conquered the Southern Song dynasty** in 1279, ending its rule over China. However, many of its inventions, ideas, and culture remain influential to this day.

Jin Dynasty
(1115–1234 CE)

The Jin dynasty took over the Northern Song dynasty in 1115 and lasted 119 years, ending in 1234. **Learn about how culture developed in the Jin dynasty** and how the dynasty finally fell apart with these twenty facts.

251. **The Jin dynasty was founded by the Jurchen people** in 1115 CE.

252. **The Jurchen were tribes that lived in northeastern China**. They were unified under Wanyan Aguda, who became **Emperor Taizu of Jin.**

253. **Emperor Taizu of Jin unified northern China after defeating rival warlords** and establishing a strong central government.

254. **He moved his capital from Huining to Yanjing** (modern-day Beijing) in 1153. He also created a southern capital, Bianjing (modern-day Kaifeng).

255. **After their conquest, about three million Jurchens migrated to China**. Although **they were the minority**, they ruled the ethnic Chinese

population of the empire, which almost outnumbered the Jurchens ten to one.

256. **After having defeated the Northern Song, the Jin dynasty chose earth as its dynastic element**. According **to the Five Elements practice of the Chinese culture**, earth comes after fire—an element that was associated with the Song—making this choice deliberate and symbolic.

257. **The Jin dynasty is credited with creating a unified currency system** by introducing paper money in 1160, replacing coins.

258. **The Jin dynasty developed differently than the Southern Song dynasty**. This was mainly because the two empires did not communicate with each other and were rivals.

259. **The Jin were known for being the first to use gunpowder effectively in warfare**, although they did not win the battle.

260. **The Jin Dynasty added to the Great Wall of China, although they built their parts of the wall differently**. They would dig a ditch and then build a wall inside of it.

261. **Under the Jin, Daoism underwent great transformations**, growing as a religion, with the dominant **Quanzhen School being founded** in the 1160s.

262. **Emperor Shizong** (r. 1161–1189) **promoted Jurchen traditions**. He declared that government officials should speak in Jurchen instead of Chinese.

263. **The emperors of the Jin dynasty had two names**. The first one was their Jurchen name, while they also adopted Chinese names and were given posthumous titles.

264. **The mighty army of the Jin dynasty was heavily comprised of mounted warriors**, something that had to do with the origins of the Jurchens.

265. **Despite its strength on land, the Jin dynasty suffered catastrophic losses at sea**, with the navy being defeated multiple times by the Song armies.

266. **The government of the Jin**, much like preceding non-Chinese rulers, **tried to adopt Chinese customs and forms of governance** while trying to combine them with Jurchen traditions.

267. Due to internal political squabbles, **the Jin dynasty declined drastically after having suffered military defeats at the hands of the Song** in the late 12th century.

268. In the 13th century, **Emperor Xuanzong decided to attack the Southern Song to assert his dominance but was defeated**, much like his ancestors about half a century before. This further contributed to the Jin dynasty's decline.

269. In 1211 CE, **Genghis Khan invaded northern China and captured Yanjing** in 1215, forcing **the Jin court into exile in Manchuria**.

270. **The Southern Song dynasty helped the Mongols take down the Jin dynasty**, which came to an end in 1234.

Yuan Dynasty
(1271–1368 CE)

The Yuan dynasty is notable for many reasons, one of which is Marco Polo's visits to China. Explore how **Mongol rule** differed from dynasties that came before, and find out why the dynasty came to its inevitable end.

271. **The Yuan dynasty was the first foreign dynasty to rule over all of China.**

272. **Kublai Khan, leader of the Mongol Empire and grandson of Genghis Khan, founded the dynasty.**

273. Chinese culture flourished in many areas. **The Four Masters of Yuan were renowned for their artwork,** with later artists trying to emulate their style.

274. **Marco Polo visited during this period** and dictated his travels to a fellow prisoner. **Rustichello da Pisa wrote the famous book** *The Travels of Marco Polo,* which helped spread knowledge about China throughout Europe.

275. Although **the stories in** *The Travels of Marco Polo* **are interesting**, they are also fantastical. Some historians believe that Marco Polo might have never stepped foot in China at all.

276. **The capital of the Yuan dynasty was Dadu** (modern-day Beijing). This was the first time Beijing was the capital of all of China.

277. **The Mongols tried to bring paper money to places outside of China,** but it was viewed as foreign, so the people didn't trust it.

278. **The Yuan dynasty supported Buddhism and Confucianism**, although many religions, including **Christianity and Islam, were practiced.**

279. **Since the Yuan dynasty was tolerant of most religions,** the number of Muslims in China rose significantly.

280. **Gunpowder weapons were used extensively by armies**. The Mongols relied on bombs and cannons to fight their enemies.

281. **Kublai Khan promoted growth on the Silk Road and provided loans to finance trade caravans**, which allowed the economy to prosper.

282. **Carrots, turnips, and cotton were some of the things that became popular during this dynasty.**

283. **The Great Wall of China was repaired and extended by Mongolian soldiers.**

284. **Tea drinking became popular** among people living in China, with tea houses established in cities like Beijing and Hangzhou.

285. **Most works were still printed with block printing**, but some were printed with moveable type. **The Mongols printed many books**, giving us many sources to examine today.

286. **The Yuan dynasty was the first to use the abacus for calculations in China.**

287. **The Mongolian language never fully supplanted Chinese**. In fact, most of the inscriptions from this period are written in both languages.

288. **The Yuan dynasty introduced a new writing system called the 'Phagspa script.** This writing system was meant to be a unified script for the lands the Mongols conquered.

289. **Despite the strength of the Mongol army at the time, Kublai Khan was unable to conquer Japan.**

His invasions in 1274 and 1281 all failed. The Japanese were able to partially stop the Mongols, but heavy storms and unfavorable conditions at sea created further problems and also contributed to their defeat.

290. **Internal problems and natural disasters led to the Yuan dynasty's decline**. When the Red Turban Rebellion broke out, the Yuan rulers were not strong enough to fight back.

Ming Dynasty
(1368–1644 CE)

It is time to explore another iconic era in Chinese history: the Ming dynasty. We will discover information about **Zheng He, religion, and weaponry.** The Ming dynasty is well known for its cultural contributions; let's find out why!

291. **The Ming dynasty was the fourth-longest dynasty in Chinese history**, stretching from 1368 to 1644 CE.

292. **Peasant rebel leader Zhu Yuanzhang founded the dynasty.** He later declared himself **the Hongwu Emperor** and established **the capital in Nanjing** in 1368.

293. **The early years of the Ming dynasty were marked by reforms**, including land distribution, tax reduction, and suppression of powerful families.

294. **Great achievements made during the Ming included advances in shipbuilding and navigation technology which allowed for explorations.** One of the most notable was Zheng He's voyages to Southeast Asia, the Middle East, and Africa between 1405 and 1433.

295. **The Chinese population increased dramatically under the rule of this dynasty.** It is hard to know the exact numbers since the population figures from this period are not exact, but some historians believe that around **two hundred million people called China home.**

296. **The modern bristle toothbrush was invented in China in 1498.**

297. **The famous Forbidden City in Beijing was built during the Ming dynasty.** The Forbidden City saw twenty-four emperors sit on its throne over a span of five hundred years.

298. **Chinese artisans were known for using vivid colors** and intricate designs, like the blue and white porcelains that this era is well known for.

299. **Buddhism, Daoism, and Confucianism were the three most important religions/philosophies during this time.** Chinese folk religions were also practiced by the people.

300. **The *Yongle Dadian*, an encyclopedia, contained thousands of volumes from all areas of study.** Most of the volumes have been lost, but it was considered the world's largest encyclopedia until Wikipedia knocked it down a peg.

301. **Gunpowder weapons were used extensively and developed by leaps and bounds.** By the end of the Ming dynasty, European-style firearms were popular.

302. Many great works of literature emerged. **Authors like Feng Menglong wrote stories about ordinary people.** Social issues played a prominent role in poems and stories during this dynasty.

303. **The Grand Canal was extended and linked with natural waterways,** allowing a sea trade route from Beijing to Hangzhou.

304. **Neo-Confucianism became very popular during the Ming dynasty,** although it later faced scrutiny. Some scholars, like **Wang Yangming, believed that people who had not experienced the real world were not as wise as those who had,** stating that peasants with real experience were wiser than officials.

305. This dynasty also saw some famous works of literature, such as *Journey to the West* and possibly *Water Margin.*

306. **Traditional forms of theater were admired by all classes,** with puppet operas being a particularly favored form of entertainment.

307. **The Ming dynasty enacted sumptuary laws, which tried to relegate how much people bought.** For instance, merchants and commoners could not wear silk.

308. **At the beginning of the Ming dynasty, the power of the eunuchs was restricted.** As time passed, more control was given to them. They built their own social structures and sometimes rivaled the emperor in power.

309. **China became increasingly isolated during the Ming dynasty, closing its borders to foreigners.**

310. **Ming rule ended in 1644 when rebel forces led by Li Zicheng overthrew the last emperor Chongzhen in Beijing.** He declared a new dynasty, which took control of the country until 1911.

Qing Dynasty
(1644–1911 CE)

Explore the fascinating history of the Qing dynasty. Learn about several famous rulers of this period, and discover the advancements that were made. The last imperial dynasty of China has much in store, so let's dive in!

311. **The Qing dynasty was the last imperial dynasty of China** and lasted from 1644 to 1911.

312. **The Manchu people, originally from northeast Asia and descended from the Jurchens, ruled the dynasty**.

313. **The Shunzhi Emperor was the second emperor of the Qing dynasty but the first to rule over all of China.** He took the throne he was only five years old!

314. **The Kangxi Emperor is considered one of the most exceptional Chinese emperors** and reigned for sixty-one years—longer than any other Chinese ruler in history!

315. During **the Kangxi Emperor's reign**, customs houses **traded with foreign countries. Open trade with the West** wouldn't happen until after **the Opium War** of 1842.

316. **The Eight Banners were military divisions, with soldiers being organized into units based on their ethnicity and social status.** The Qing dynasty relied on them for military campaigns, but over time, the Eight Banners stopped being an effective fighting force.

317. **Emperor Qianlong had an exceedingly successful reign**. Historians believe the Qing dynasty was at the height of its power during his rule.

318. He commissioned **the largest collection of Chinese books** that we know of, **the *Siku Quanshu* or the *Complete Repository of the Four Branches of Literature***. It included almost thirty-seven thousand volumes!

319. **During this period, China's contact with the outside world increased dramatically**. European powers, such as **Russia and Great Britain**, colonized parts of China and bordering regions, leading to territorial disputes that would last for centuries.

320. **The opium trade between British India and Qing-ruled provinces created immense profits** for merchants and caused chaos in many parts of the country due to drug addiction.

321. **Emperor Tongzhi attempted to modernize China during his reign with Western technologies**, such as railroads, telegraph systems, hospitals, and schools. He died before he could finish it.

322. **Empress Dowager Cixi was the one who came up with the idea of modernizing China,** as the country needed a boost to survive.

323. **Although Empress Dowager Cixi never officially ruled in name**, she was a regent and ensured her nephew sat on the throne after her son died so she could maintain power.

324. **Empress Dowager Cixi did not approve of Western governance,** but she did think that some Western reforms would help strengthen the country. By the end of her life, she began to embrace the idea of a constitutional monarchy.

325. **Han Chinese men were required to wear their hair in a pigtail called a queue**, which was how the Manchu men wore their hair. The Han Chinese hated this law, as it reminded them that they were no longer in control of China.

326. **The Kangxi Emperor tried to put a stop to foot binding**, but he was unsuccessful. Foot binding would only be banned in 1912.

327. **The Qing dynasty saw an increase in literacy rates due to widespread education** initiatives, which, in turn, led to great works of literature being devoured by the populace.

328. One famous piece of literature was *Dream of the Red Chamber*. This book has been studied extensively and even has its own field of study called **Redology!**

329. **Confucianism was promoted by many emperors,** but its emphasis on social harmony and obedience to authority hindered technological progress and progressive policies, things that were taking place elsewhere in the world.

330. **The Chinese inoculated against smallpox and saw a decrease** in the infant mortality rate because of advances in medicine.

331. **Women began to write more during this period**. They mostly wrote poetry.

332. At the height **of the Qing rule, China was so powerful** that it forced many of its neighboring states to pay tribute.

333. **Tea was China's biggest export**. In the early 19th century, tea accounted for 90 percent of exports out of Canton.

334. **The Yongzheng Emperor banned Christianity**. He also started programs to help combat famine and poverty in rural regions.

335. **Calligraphy and painting remained popular pursuits**. The Four Wangs were prominent painters from this period.

336. **Railroads were introduced to China** for the first time during the Qing dynasty.

337. **The series of reforms** that attempted to pursue modernization in the late 19th century would be referred to as **the "Self-Strengthening Movement."** The reforms impacted some of the most important aspects of life, such as the economy, military, and education.

338. **Empress Dowager Longyu declared an end to imperial rule** on February 12th, 1911, on behalf of the six-year-old emperor, Puyi.

339. In 1917, **Zhang Xun tried to restore the Qing dynasty,** but he failed.

340. **Puyi would later become the puppet emperor of the Japanese**-controlled state of Manchukuo, which fell at the end of World War II.

The Opium Wars
(1839–1842, 1856–1860 CE)

The Opium Wars were fought between China and various Western powers, namely Britain. Why did they start? What did they accomplish? We will take a look at these questions and uncover some other interesting facts along the way.

341. **The First Opium War was a war between China and Britain**, which lasted from 1839 to 1842.

342. **It started because the Chinese government wanted to end the opium trade**. Opium is a drug made from poppy plants. The British did not want to end such a lucrative trade.

343. **During the war, several battles were fought**. The Chinese war junks, a type of ship with sails, were often overpowered by the British navy, which possessed larger ships with cannons mounted on them.

344. **After almost three years of fighting, Britain won the war** due to its superior weapons and military technology compared to China's forces.

345. **China had to give up Hong Kong Island to Britain**. It also **had to open ports in Guangdong Province** so British merchants could legally sell opium there without restrictions.

346. **This significant event caused tensions between Chinese citizens and foreign governments.** These tensions are still felt to this day.

347. **The Treaty of Nanking, which ended the First Opium War**, was the first of what are called unequal treaties. These treaties gave more power and control to Western powers while granting China very little in return.

348. Opium is highly addictive. The Treaty of Nanking did not include any provisions to address the problem. It is believed the number of opium addicts nearly doubled after the treaty was signed.

349. The Second Opium War started because of a dispute over trading rights, and it involved not only Britain but also France and other Western powers.

350. In October 1860, **the Summer Palace was looted by British and French soldiers**. Priceless works of art were taken to Europe.

351. **The Second Opium War ended with the signing of the Treaty of Tientsin** (1858) and the Convention of Peking (1860). These treaties further expanded trade privileges for Western powers, legalized the opium trade, and led to more territorial concessions for China.

352. **The Opium Wars contributed greatly to the decline of China as a regional and world power**, turning it into almost a semi-colonized state.

353. **By 1870, China's global GDP had fallen by half**. Historians believe the drop was a direct consequence of the Opium Wars.

354. **The Opium Wars were the first precedent of the unfair relationship** that would eventually develop between the industrialized West and 19th-century China, which was trailing behind in technological and social advancements.

355. Despite the West's victory, **many critiqued the Opium Wars for their imperialist nature and the domination of the Chinese by the Europeans**. Criticisms came from intellectuals, such as Karl Marx, who condemned the West's actions in the war.

Taiping Rebellion
(1850–1864 CE)

This section will explore the fascinating **Taiping Rebellion**, one of the most important events in **the Qing dynasty**. We'll look at ten interesting facts about its leader and his followers' beliefs. We'll also discover **the changes that this rebellion brought** about.

356. **The Taiping Rebellion was a civil war in China** that lasted from 1850 to 1864.

357. **It was fought between the Qing dynasty**, which ruled China, and a rebel group called **the Taiping Heavenly Kingdom**.

358. **Hong Xiuquan, the commander of the rebellion**, believed God had chosen him to lead his people out of suffering and poverty. He actually said that he was the brother of Jesus Christ.

359. Though the exact number of casualties is disputed, **it is believed that at least twenty million people died during the Taiping Rebellion,** making it one of the bloodiest events in recent Chinese history.

360. **The Taiping Rebellion is the bloodiest civil war in history**. Both sides engaged in massacres against the other, although most deaths happened because of disease and famine.

361. **The success of the rebels varied from year to year**, but the Qing government was eventually able to suppress the rebellion. This was partially due to the rebels' lack of organization, as well as reluctance from foreign powers to aid them.

362. During its peak, **the Taiping Heavenly Kingdom controlled over half of modern-day China,** including major cities like Nanjing (once known as Nanking).

363. **Women played an essential role in this rebellion**. They served as soldiers, nurses, and even generals in **the Taiping army**. It was rare for women to serve in a fighting capacity at this point in the 19th century, making the Taiping army unique.

364. **Although this rebellion was one of the factors responsible for imperial China's decline,** it also gave the Chinese emperors a chance to strengthen China so it could stand strong on the world stage.

365. **The rebellion led to important short-term changes in Chinese society**, such **as Han officials gaining more power in government.** Provincial armies became more important, replacing the imperial forces. These would play a factor in the eventual end of the Qing dynasty.

Tongzhi Restoration
(1860–1874 CE)

Let's uncover **ten amazing facts about the Tongzhi Restoration**. Improvements were made to many areas of Chinese society and government, **which helped to strengthen China** and bring it more into the modern era.

366. **The Tongzhi Restoration was a period in China that lasted from 1860 to 1874.**

367. During this time, **the Chinese government worked to restore order and stability** after years of civil wars and foreign invasions.

368. The name of this period was derived from the title of **the Tongzhi Emperor,** who ruled from 1861 to 1875.

369. Although the period was named after **the Tongzhi Emperor, it was his mother, Empress Dowager Cixi, who came up with the ideas of how to make China strong** once more.

370. **Many reforms were made during this era**, including improvements to education, transportation systems, military organization, and taxation policies. **These reforms helped strengthen the Chinese economy and society.**

371. **The Tongzhi Restoration opened a foreign office to deal with diplomats**, which helped open China up more to other countries.

372. **Although the Tongzhi Restoration did modernize some things**, Empress Dowager Cixi clung to the old traditions. Historians believe this caused the period not to reach its full potential.

373. **For the most part, the reforms did not reach their full potential** because the government was unsure how to implement them.

374. **China reformed its military during this time**, but it was unable to score a decisive victory in **the Sino-Japanese War**.

375. **The Tongzhi Restoration did help strengthen traditional Chinese values**, which brought some unity to the country.

The First Sino-Japanese War
(1894–1895)

Japan and China both sought to be the major power in the East. The tensions between the two finally exploded with **the First Sino-Japanese War**. Let's look at ten facts about this war and how it impacted China.

376. **The First Sino-Japanese War was fought between July 1894 and April 1895 over Korea.**

377. **Korea had long been under China's sphere of influence**. In 1876, Korea was opened up to trade with Japan.

378. **Japan worried that Korea was too underdeveloped.** The Japanese government believed that if Korea was unable to defend itself, Western powers would swoop in and take it over.

379. **When China sent forces to help put down the Tonghak Rebellion in Korea**, Japan claimed it violated a previous treaty, which eventually led to a declaration of war.

380. **China also had to deal with a rebellion in northern China while fighting the First Sino-Japanese War**. Chinese Muslims rebelled against the Qing government because it refused to declare which Sufi order was superior.

381. **The Qing dynasty was forced to sue for peace after six months of warfare.**

382. **China was no longer the dominant power in East Asia**, as Japan had emerged as the clear winner of the war.

383. **China lost around thirty-five thousand men** (dead and wounded), while Japan suffered around five thousand casualties.

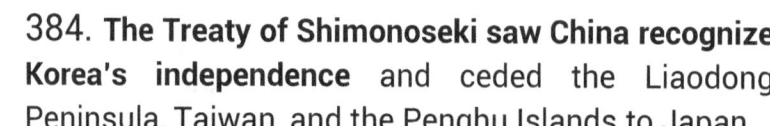

384. **The Treaty of Shimonoseki saw China recognize Korea's independence** and ceded the Liaodong Peninsula, Taiwan, and the Penghu Islands to Japan.

385. **Japan would go on to invade Taiwan in 1895 since a number of officials refused to recognize the treaty and instead set up a democratic republic**. Japan was eventually able to annex the island.

Boxer Rebellion
(1899–1901 CE)

Discover **the story of the Boxer Rebellion**, a two-year conflict in China between foreign powers and Chinese rebels. This chapter **will explore ten interesting facts about this rebellion**, from its origins to its eventual defeat.

386. **The Boxer Rebellion was a rebellion in China against foreign influence and control.**

387. **It started when Chinese people formed the Society of Righteous and Harmonious Fists,** an organization to fight against foreigners taking over their country.

388. Since many of **the rebels practiced martial arts, the English called them "Boxers."** The name must have stuck!

389. During the rebellion, **the Boxers attacked foreign embassies, churches, and businesses across China** but primarily in Beijing (the capital of China).

390. **To put down the rebellion, eight countries sent troops to help defeat the rebels.** These countries were **Japan, Russia, Britain, Germany, Austria-Hungary, Italy, the US, and France.**

391. **After two years of fighting, the international forces defeated the Boxers in 1901,** but it took another decade to fully restore peace between China and the other nations and to address the domestic issues caused by the rebellion.

392. **Any government official who supported the Boxers was executed,** and China was forced to pay a huge indemnity to the eight-nation alliance.

393. **Empress Dowager Cixi, who was still the main power behind the throne, supported the Boxers.** Later, she made nice with the Western powers, agreeing to make changes that would **turn the country into a constitutional monarchy.**

394. **The Qing dynasty tried to repair the damage created by the Boxers,** but the dynasty was weakened. The reforms that it tried to enact were not enough, leading to **the end of the monarchy in 1911.**

395. **Although Western powers played a big role in the Boxer Rebellion, Japan emerged as the dominant power.** In time, Japan would control a good chunk of East Asia, including parts of China.

The 1911 Revolution
(1911–1912 CE)

The 1911 Revolution was a pivotal moment in human history. **The Qing dynasty was overthrown, ending the imperial rule of China.** Discover what took the monarchy's place and other interesting trivia about this revolution with these fifteen enthralling facts.

396. **Another name for the 1911 Revolution is the Xinhai Revolution**. It is named after the year it took place on **the Chinese calendar**.

397. **Although the 1911 Revolution was successful**, it was far from the first uprising to rock China in the late 19th and early 20th centuries.

398. **Sun Yat-sen, the leader of the 1911 Revolution**, participated in many of the earlier uprisings.

399. **In 1894, Sun Yat-sen formed the Revive China Society** (Xingzhonghui). A year later, another prominent rebel group, **the Furen Literary Society**, merged with the Revive China Society.

400. **Sun Yat-sen was in exile during this time**; he created his revolutionary party in Honolulu, Hawaii.

401. **In 1905, the Revive China Society would transform into the Kuomintang or KMT**. This is still a major political party in China today.

402. Although uprisings had occurred in previous years, **the Wuchang Uprising in October 1911 is considered the event that kicked off the 1911 Revolution.** Other regions soon followed, with people fighting against the Qin dynasty.

403. In 1911, **Yuan Shikai, a military official, was appointed prime minister by the Qing dynasty** to deal with the rebels.

404. **The Republic of China was created in January 1912. Sun Yat-sen would become its first president.**

405. **Sun Yat-sen would be president for a little over two months**. Yuan Shikai would become president in March.

406. **To become president, Yuan Shikai had to get Emperor Puyi to abdicate.** Since the emperor was so young (he was only six), his regent, **Empress Dowager Longyu, had to sign the papers for him.**

407. **Life did not change much for the average Chinese**. The biggest thing that changed was the abolishment of feudalism.

408. **There was a lot of anti-Manchu sentiment after the revolution. In Beijing**, thousands of Manchu people died in violent attacks.

409. **Four thousand years of imperial rule ended when the Qing dynasty was overthrown.**

410. **As time passed, the Chinese became divided again**, with some seeing the 1911 Revolution as the final stage for a democratic China and others seeing it as a stepping stone for a greater revolution.

Yuan Shikai's Attempt to Reestablish Imperial Rule

(1915–1916)

Although **Yuan Shikai became president of China**, he wasn't content with the level of power he was given. **He wanted to return back to the monarchy**. Let's look at five interesting facts about his reign, including how **he declared himself emperor** and why his attempt failed.

411. **Yuan Shikai quickly secured power as president**, which allowed him to gather support when he wanted to return to **the traditional way of ruling**. In December 1915, he was elected emperor.

412. **Yuan Shikai became known as the Hongxian Emperor**.

413. **The revolutionaries did not like this move, and neither did Yuan Shikai's military officials.** The people rebelled, and when **Yuan Shikai did not perform well in the battles**, he lost foreign support.

414. **Yuan Shikai only ruled for eighty-three days.**

415. **When he died in June 1916, his death left a power vacuum**, with many warlords racing to fill it themselves.

Warlord Era
(1916–1928 CE)

Discover **the turbulent history of China during the Warlord Era**. This chapter will explore five interesting facts about this period, including how it finally ended.

416. **The Warlord Era was a time of chaos and conflict in China**, as many different warlords fought for control of the country.

417. **The main fight was between the Kuomintang government's army and Yuan Shikai's former government's army**, although other groups rose up as well.

418. The biggest battle of this period was **the Central Plains War**. Over one million soldiers fought in it!

419. **The Warlord Era ended with the Northern Expedition**, led by **Chiang Kai-shek**, in 1928, which united most of China under one rule again.

420. **Warlords continued to pop up and create serious threats for the next few decades**, which added to China's instability.

Chinese Civil War
(1927–1949 CE)

This chapter will explore **the tumultuous history of the Chinese Civil War**. Explore ten interesting facts about this conflict, including how it was fought and who ultimately won.

421. **The Chinese Civil War was a conflict between the Communist Party of China and the Nationalist** (Kuomintang) Party of China.

422. **It lasted from 1927 to 1949**, although there was a break in the fighting when **the Chinese put aside their differences to fight Japan** and aid the Allies in World War II.

423. There are no exact records of how many died, but **millions of people were killed or displaced due to fighting** and famine.

424. **The Communist Party of China was supported by the Soviet Union**, while **the Nationalist Party of China received support from the United States** and other Western countries.

425. **As the years passed, the communist forces gained more followers**. By 1945, they had over three million troops at their command.

426. **The Chinese Civil War resumed in 1946 when Chiang Kai-shek led an assault on northern China.**

427. Both sides committed war crimes. **The Nationalist forces conducted the White Terror, killing hundreds of thousands of people who were suspected of being communists.** The communist forces targeted landlords, as they wanted to redistribute the land to the peasants.

428. In October 1949, **Mao Zedong's communist forces won control over most of mainland China and established the People's Republic of China** (PRC).

429. **Chiang Kai-shek and around two million Nationalist soldiers retreated to Taiwan**, where their government, **the Republic of China** (ROC), was formed.

430. **The Republic of China laid claim to China proper until 1988. The People's Republic of China claims sovereignty of Taiwan**, even though it has never controlled any part of it.

The Second Sino-Japanese War
(1937–1945)

The Second Sino-Japanese War was a devastating conflict that is often overshadowed by World War II. This section takes a look at how the war began and some of the atrocities that were committed.

431. **The Second Sino-Japanese War took place from 1937 to 1945.** The war is sometimes **called the Asian Holocaust.**

432. **Japan invaded Manchuria in 1931 and eventually established a puppet state called Manchukuo,** which was headed by **Emperor Puyi, the last Qing emperor.**

433. **In July 1937, a Japanese force demanded entry into Wanping, near Beijing,** to look for a missing soldier. The Chinese stationed there refused. Shots were eventually fired. Many see this as the beginning of **the Second Sino-Japanese War.**

434. **During the Second Sino-Japanese War, around twenty million people were killed.** Most of them were civilians.

435. **This war is notable for the Nanjing massacre, also known as the Rape of Nanjing.** The massacre lasted around six weeks and saw anywhere between 40,000 and 300,000 civilians die.

436. **Looting, rape, arson, and murder took place during those six weeks.** Some in Japan downplay the incident, with some even claiming the event never took place. **Japan has yet to apologize for the massacre,** which is a source of tension to this day.

437. **By 1939, the Japanese controlled most of China's larger cities,** but they could not advance much in the countryside, where members of **the Chinese Communist Party used guerilla tactics to keep the Japanese at bay.**

438. **When Japan attacked Pearl Harbor in 1941, the US increased its aid to China.** The US gave China around twenty billion dollars in today's money, giving the Chinese a fighting chance against the Japanese forces.

439. **In 1945, Japan surrendered because of the atomic bombings of Hiroshima and Nagasaki.** China regained its lost territories **and became a permanent member of the UN Security Council.**

440. **Once World War II ended, the Chinese Civil War continued,** with the Communists eventually winning.

People's Republic of China
(1949–Present)

The People's Republic of China is often in the news today, but how much do you know about it? These fifteen interesting facts will give you a better idea of the PRC in general; the next few sections will take a look at its history.

441. **The People's Republic of China was founded in 194**9 and is **the second-most populous country in the world after India**, with over 1.4 billion people living there.

442. **Today, China has twenty-three provinces, five autonomous regions, four direct-controlled municipalities, and two Special Administrative Regions** (SARs). The two SARs are Hong Kong and Macau.

443. **Beijing is China's capital city**. It is China's **second-largest city** in terms of population, with **Shanghai being the first**.

444. **Mandarin Chinese is the official language used in both China and Taiwan**, although other dialects are spoken.

445. Although **China is an atheist state**, it **recognizes four religions: Daoism, Buddhism, Islam, and Christianity.**

446. **Confucianism isn't regarded as a religion by most**, although its teachings are still celebrated today.

447. **China has many UNESCO World Heritage Sites** that preserve its rich cultural past.

448. **Peking duck, dumplings, and noodles are all popular dishes in traditional Chinese restaurants.**

449. **China has more billionaires than any other country besides the United States.**

450. **Chinese have to attend school for at least nine years**. Many go on to attend university.

451. **As of 2023, China is the most popular country in Asia** for international students looking to receive a higher education degree.

452. **In 2013, China became the world's largest trading nation**. Most of what China trades is electronics and clothing.

453. **Giant pandas have become an unofficial symbol of China because China would gift pandas as a way to establish diplomatic relations**. Giant pandas are native to China. The pandas you see in zoos are on loan from China, so they technically belong to the Chinese government.

454. **Chinese currency is called renminbi or people's currency**. Most nations outside of China call it **the yuan**, which is the basic unit of **the renminbi**.

455. **China has become one of the largest economies in recent years** due to its booming manufacturing industry.

Cultural Revolution
(1966–1976)

The Cultural Revolution of China sought to preserve communism in China. However, it **has been criticized for causing the nation distress**. Let's look at ten facts about this period to see what happened.

456. **The Cultural Revolution in China was a time of notable change** and upheaval, lasting from 1966 to 1976. **Mao Zedong was the leader of China** during this time.

457. **The Red Guards, which were student military organizations, were encouraged to destroy historical artifacts** and architecture so the people wouldn't be reminded of the past.

458. **People had their personal belongings searched by Red Guards** when they were accused of being traitors or enemies of communism. There could be deadly consequences for those found guilty.

459. **Artistic expression was heavily censored during this period**. Books, films, music, and theater performances that did not promote communist ideals were banned or drastically altered before being released into public circulation.

460. **Millions of Chinese citizens left for other countries** due to political turmoil caused by the revolution's harsh policies.

461. **Many massacres took place. The Guangxi massacre saw tens of thousands of people die in cruel ways.** Cannibalism was even encouraged by local communist officials. There was no famine; people were motivated to do this for political reasons.

462. **People belonging to the Five Black Categories were considered enemies of the state.** These categories were landlords, counter-revolutionaries, rich farmers, "bad elements," and people belonging to conservative parties.

463. **Even senior government officials were accused of betraying China. Liu Shaoqi**, who had served as chairman of the PRC from 1959 to 1968, was accused of supporting capitalism. He died in prison.

464. **Intellectuals were persecuted, and universities were shut down**. Opportunities for rural-educated children rose, while those in the cities, especially those belonging to wealthier families, saw fewer opportunities to advance.

465. **The Cultural Revolution continued after Mao's death, ending with the arrest of the Gang of Four**, a group that held significant sway during **the Cultural Revolution**.

Reform and Opening-up
(1978–Present)

This chapter will explore **the remarkable transformation of Chinese society** since 1978. Discover fifteen amazing facts about how this period impacted China's economy and society.

466. In 1978, **the Reform and Opening-up period took place** when China started opening its economy to other countries.

467. **This period allowed people to buy more things**, start businesses, and travel abroad for the first time in many years!

468. **There has been a consistent decline in the number of Chinese people living in poverty** since 1978.

469. **Foreign investment has grown significantly over the past few decades**, helping create jobs in China's cities and rural areas.

470. **Farmers were allowed to sell their produce directly to markets** instead of going through government-run stores, which helped increase incomes drastically.

471. **There have also been notable improvements** in healthcare coverage and educational opportunities in China since the reforms began.

472. **In 1979, Deng Xiaoping introduced the one country, two systems approach**, which allowed **Hong Kong and Macau to have a different economic and political system** than China proper.

473. In 1984, **fourteen Special Economic Zones were set up** in coastal cities to encourage foreign investment. These areas have rapidly developed into some of the most prosperous regions in China today.

474. **Reforms also included creating more effective legal systems**, increasing religious freedom, and allowing people more personal freedoms, such as choice over marriage partners and careers.

475. As part of its reform efforts, **China has signed bilateral agreements like trade deals with other countries,** becoming an increasingly active member of the international community.

476. **China is one of the largest economies globally by GDP**. Some analysts believe **it will take over the US** in about a decade.

477. **The Chinese government has invested heavily in research and development**, coming up with many new inventions **in technology and medicine.**

478. **China is the world's largest exporter**, with exports of over $2 trillion in 2018. This was only made possible with the reforms that started in 1978.

479. In recent years, **China has become a key player in digital technology, including artificial intelligence and blockchain,** which are considered essential tools for future economic development.

480. **The Reform and Opening-up period changed Chinese society dramatically** by creating new opportunities while improving living standards across the country.

Tiananmen Square Protests
(1989 CE)

The Tiananmen Square protests of 1989 have gone down in history as one of the most iconic moments for democratic movements. These five facts will provide some basic information about what happened.

481. **On June 4th, 1989, a peaceful protest happened in Tiananmen Square in China** to call for more freedom and democracy.

482. **The Chinese government sent troops to break up the protest**. They did so violently, with thousands dead and wounded.

483. **History may never know how many people actually died**, as the Chinese government refuses to release the official

figures. **The official number is three hundred deaths**, but eyewitness accounts place the number much higher.

484. **The protests were largely influenced by Hu Yaobang's death**. He was a pro-reform politician who was forced to resign, dying shortly after his resignation because of a heart attack.

485. **One of the most iconic images of the 20th century took place during the protests when the picture of one man standing in front of a line of tanks was captured**. It is unknown what happened to this man.

Rise of China
(1990s—Present)

This chapter will explore the remarkable history and development of China from 1990 to the present day. These fifteen facts will provide some hard data as to how far China has come.

486. By today's standards, **China is one of the most modern countries in the world**. According to the 2017 statistics, all of its population has access to electricity.

487. From 1979 to 2017, **China's economy grew at an average rate of 10 percent**, making it one of the fastest-growing economies in history.

488. Since 1990, **notable advancements in healthcare have happened**. Infant mortality rates decreased, and life expectancy increased.

489. Since 1979, **over seven hundred million Chinese have escaped poverty due to economic growth** and reforms implemented by the government.

490. **China joined the World Trade Organization** (WTO) in 2001, which opened up its markets for international trade, leading to increased foreign investment and growth opportunities for businesses within its borders.

491. **China's space program achieved a milestone by launching the first Chinese into orbit aboard a Shenzhou-5 in 2003.** The country continues to make strides in space exploration.

492. **China is a permanent member of the UN's Security Council**. This once again proves the country's international importance.

493. **The Belt and Road Initiative** (BRI**) launched by President Xi Jinping** in 2013 aims to bring together more than 150 countries by cooperating on large-scale infrastructure projects. **China is looking to take on more of a leadership role** with this initiative.

494. **Although China has made much progress, there is still much work to be done**. In recent years, **China has been accused of human rights violations**, particularly **against the Uyghurs.**

495. **In addition, one of the biggest problems modern China is facing has to do with pollution**. Compared to other big countries, it still lacks green infrastructure and is the world's largest polluter of air.

496. In 2021, **China invested a record-breaking $378 billion in research and development projects**, advancing its technology and innovation capacity.

497. **High-speed railways are crisscrossing long distances at record speeds**, while motorways connect different cities like never before.

498. **Chinese citizens have greater access to technology** due to rapid developments in 5G network capabilities and internet infrastructure.

499. **As wealth has spread across China, cities have seen notable growth**, with towering skyscrapers appearing in Shanghai and Beijing.

500. Over the past thirty years, **the Chinese government has made great strides toward improving their standard of living** and creating jobs and new opportunities for future generations.

Conclusion

Our journey through Chinese history has been long but fascinating. We have **seen great dynasties rise and fall**, periods of **turmoil and revolution**, and times of peace and prosperity. We have witnessed warlords, civil unrest, and **massive social reforms.**

China's remarkable rise on the world stage is likely to continue, and the nation will undoubtedly continue to be in the news in the decades to come. **China has made great strides toward improving the people's lives,** although there is still much criticism by other countries over how the government operates.

This book has offered readers a look at some key facts that shaped Chinese history. Hopefully, some of these facts were new to you. And hopefully this book has piqued your interest into **reading more about China's fascinating past.**

Check out another book in the series

Welcome Aboard, Check Out This Limited-Time Free Bonus!

Ahoy, reader! Welcome to the Ahoy Publications family, and thanks for snagging a copy of this book! Since you've chosen to join us on this journey, we'd like to offer you something special.

Check out the link below for a FREE e-book filled with delightful facts about American History.

But that's not all - you'll also have access to our exclusive email list with even more free e-books and insider knowledge. Well, what are ye waiting for? Visit the link below to join and set sail toward exciting adventures in American History.

To access your limited-time free bonus, go to: ahoypublications.com/

Sources and Additional References

"Zhou Dynasty Rulers." History Today, www.historytoday.com/zhoudynastyrulers/316517, Accessed October 26 2020.

"Social Structure in Ancient China," World History Encyclopedia, https://www.worldhistory.encyclopedia.com/socialstructure/ancient/china/html, Accessed October 26 2020.

The Editors of Encyclopedia Britannica. "Pre-Imperial China." Encyclopedia Britannica, Encyclopedia Britannica, Inc., 24 June 2019, www.britannica.com/topic/pre-imperial-China#ref863156.

Smith, Mark J., ed. "Confucius." Ancient History Encyclopedia 05 Aug 2012: n pag Web 09 September 2020 https://www.ancienthistoryencyclopedia.

"Writing." Ancient China for Kids, The Oriental Institute of the University of Chicago, https://oi.uchicago.edu/research/learn-about-ancient-china/life-ancient-china/writing/.

Gannett, Rachel. "Ancient Chinese Astronomy and Mathematics: Astrolabes and Tally Sticks – Ancient History Encyclopedia." Ancient History Encyclopedia, 28 July 2017, https://www.ancient.eu/article/1082/.

"Great Wall of China: Construction & Building of the Great Wall – HISTORY." HISTORY, A&E Television Networks, 13 Dec 2019, https://www.history.com/topics/great-wall-of-china/great-wall-of-china#:~:text=The%20construction%20and%20repair%20of,by%201025).

"Early Preimperial China". The Metropolitan Museum of Art, https ://www.metmuseum.org/toah/hd/epc_3/hd_epc_3.htm (accessed April 10th 2020).

"The Invention of Paper." Science Museum, https://www.sciencemuseumgroup.org.uk/articles/the-invention-of-paper/.

Sun Tzu, and Thomas Cleary (trans.). The Art of War: Translation and Commentary by Thomas Cleary / Sun Tzu; Foreword by John Minford; Afterword & Notes on Sources by Roger Ames / Shambhala Classics., Shambhala Publications [distributor], 2016.

"The I Ching or Book of Changes" The Internet Sacred Text Archive Home Page, sacredtextsarchiveorg/.

"Agricultural Production in Ancient China: The Great Inventions." Ancient History Encyclopedia, 27 Mar. 2020, www.ancient.eu/article/1401/.

"Qin Shi Huang: The First Emperor." History, A&E Television Networks, 2020, www.history.com/topics/ancient-history/qin-shi-huang#section_5.

"The Han Dynasty." Ancient History Encyclopedia, 19 Feb. 2019, www.ancient.eu/Han_Dynasty/.

Kallen, Stuart A. "The Han Dynasty." Encyclopedia Britannica, https://www.britannica.com/topic/Han-dynasty-Chinese-history. Accessed 27 June 2020.

Lewis, Mark Edward. *The Early Chinese Empires: Qin and Han*. Harvard University Press, 2007.

"The Great Wall of China | Overview & Facts | Britannica" Encyclopedia Britannica, Encyclopedia Britannica Inc., 23 June 2020, www.britannica.com/topic/Great -Wall -of -China.

Qian, Sima. *The Records of the Grand Historian*. Columbia University Press, 1974.

Cao, Biography.com Editors. "Cao Cao." Biography. A&E Television Networks, 2018.

Liu Bei biography: Liu Bei – Ancient History Encyclopedia https://www.ancienthistoryencyclopediaorg/liu-bei/(Accessed 14 June 2020).

"Jin Dynasty (265–420)." Encyclopedia Britannica; accessed June 20th 2021; https://www.britannica.com/topic/Jin-dynasty-Chinese-history.

"The Warring States Period," Ancient China, accessed June 8, 2021, https://www.ancient.eu/Warring_States_Period/.

"Sixteen Kingdoms." Britannica, The Editors of Encyclopedia Britannica, https://www.britannica.com/topic/Sixteen-Kingdoms.

"The Period of Northern and Southern Dynasties (420-589 CE)." Ancient History Encyclopedia, Ancient History Encyclopedia, 7 July 2017, www.ancient.eu/Northern_and_Southern_Dynasties/.

Turner Jr., William C. "Sui Dynasty (589–618 CE)." Khan Academy, Khan Academy, khanacademy.org/humanities/world-history/ancient-medieval/sui--tang--song-dynasties-(400ce---1200ce)/v/the--sui—dynasty.

"Grand Canal (China)." Encyclopedia Britannica, Encyclopedia Britannica, Inc., 23 Apr 2021, https://www.britannica.com/topic/Grand-Canal-China#ref406020

"Sui Dynasty (581–618)." Encyclopedia Britannica, https://www.britannica.com/topic/Sui-dynasty. Accessed 27 Apr 2021.

"The Tang Dynasty (618–907 CE)." Ancient History Encyclopedia, ancient.eu/Tang_Dynasty/.

"Women in the Tang Dynasty." Asia Society Museum Education Center for Arts & Culture, asiasocietymuseumedcenterforartscultureedu/womeninthetanddynasty. Accessed 18 Nov 2020.

Shaughnessy, Edward L., ed. *The Cambridge History of Ancient China: From the Origins of Civilization to 221 B.C.* Cambridge University Press, 1999.

Murphey, Rhoads. "Eunuchs and Power in Ming China" University of South Carolina Press, 2009-.www.uscpressedusccmceunuch.html>.

"The Five Dynasties and Ten Kingdoms Period." Ancient History Encyclopedia, ancient.eu/five_dynasties_and_ten_kingdoms/.

"Western Xia Dynasty | Chinese History | Britannica." Encyclopedia Britannica, www.britannica.com/place/Western-Xia-dynasty#ref1060483/.

"History of Acupuncture." Healthline Media UK Ltd., 2019, healthline.com/health/history − ofacupuncture.

"Liao Dynasty." Encyclopedia Britannica, Encyclopedia Britannica, Inc., 15 Apr. 2020, www.britannica.com/topic/Liao-Dynasty#ref879107.

Ebrey, Patricia Buckley. *The Cambridge Illustrated History of China* (Cambridge Illustrated Histories). Cambridge University Press; 2 edition (August 30, 1999).

"Song Dynasty." Encyclopedia Britannica, www.britannica.com/topic/Song-dynasty.

"Genghis Khan and the Mongol Conquest of China - Asia for Educators - Columbia University." Accessed May 8, 2021.

https://afe.easia.columbia.edu/mongols/pop_genghisconquestchinapowerpointless onplan2_.htm

"Silk Road," National Geographic, https://www.nationalgeographic.org/topics/exploration-and-adventure/silk-road/.

"Yuan Dynasty." Ancient History Encyclopedia, ancient.eu/yuan_dynasty/.

"Kublai Khan." Encyclopedia Britannica, www.britannica.com/biography/Kublai-Khan.

"The Travels of Marco Polo." The British Library, www.bl.uk/collectionitems/the-travels-of-marco-polo.

"Ming Dynasty." Encyclopedia Britannica, https://www.britannica.com/topic/Ming-dynasty#ref83635.

"Qing Dynasty (1644−1911)." Encyclopedia Britannica, Encyclopedia Britannica, Inc., https://www.britannica.com/place/Qing-dynasty.

Beasley, William G. "Manchu People" Encyclopedia Britannica, Encyclopedia Britannica, Inc., 8 Oct 2012, https://www.britannica.com/topic/Manchu-people#ref630815.

"Sino-European Trade". Asian Art Museum, Asian Art Museum San Francisco, http://www.asianartmuseum.org/documents/lessonplan_chinatrade.pdf

"Emperor Tongzhi." Encyclopedia Britannica, https://www.britannica.com/biography/Tongzhi-emperor-of-China. Accessed 7 Apr 2021

"Empress Cixi of China." Biography, A&E Television Networks LLC., 29 October 2016, https://www.biography.com/royalty/empress-cixi-of-china Accessed 7 April 2021.

"The Opium War (1839-1842)." History, www.history.com/topics/opium-wars/.

Hanes III, W Travis and Frank Sanello. *The Opium Wars: The Addiction of One Empire and the Corruption of Another*. Sourcebooks Trade Paperback Edition (October 1st

2002).

MacGillivray, Donald. "The Tongzhi Restoration (1862-1908)." Encyclopedia Britannica, 16 Apr. 2021, www.britannica.com/topic/Tongzhi-restoration.

"The Boxer Rebellion." History.com, A&E Television Networks, 2020, www.history.com/topics/19th-century/boxer-rebellion#:~:text=In%20late%201900s%20China,overthrow%20foreigners'ruleinChina.

Belenky, Alexander M., and Mark Czarnecki, eds. *The Chinese Revolution of 1911: A Brief History with Documents*, Bedford St Martin's (2017).

"Republican Revolution in China," Encyclopedia Britannica Online Academic Edition, accessed March 6 2021 https://www.britannica.com/event/Republican-Revolution#ref495887.

"Kuomintang." Encyclopedia Britannica, https://www.britannica.com/topic/Kuomintang-Nationalist-Party-of-China#ref302070.

"Chinese Civil War." Encyclopedia Britannica, Encyclopedia Britannica, Inc., 10 Mar. 2021, https://www.britannica.com/event/Chinese-Civil-War.

"Chiang Kai Shek and the Nationalists in China | Asia for Educators | Columbia University." Accessed 11 March 2021 http://afe.easia.columbia.edu/special/china_1900_chiangkaishek.htm.

"The People's Republic of China." The World Factbook, Central Intelligence Agency, 2019, www.cia.gov/library/publications/the-world-factbook/geos/ch.html

"The Cultural Revolution: Political Campaign Launched by Mao Zedong 1966–1976." The Cultural Revolution: Political Campaign Launched by Mao Zedong 1966–1976 | Britannica, www.britannica.com/event/Cultural-Revolution#ref351884.

"Tiananmen Square Protests." History.com, A&E Television Networks, 2 Nov. 2009, www.history.com/topics/tiananmen-square-protests.

www.ingramcontent.com/pod-product-compliance
Lightning Source LLC
Chambersburg PA
CBHW081005140626
46546CB00019B/3429